# CONFLICT FOR CIVILIZATION: THE FALLACY OF GRIEVANCE BASED TERRORISM

The consistent need to find explanations other than religious ones for the attacks says, in fact, more about the West than it does about the jihadis. Western scholars have generally failed to take religion seriously. Secularists, whether liberals or socialists, grant true explanatory power to political, social or economic factors but discount the plain sense of religious statements made by the jihadis themselves. To see why jihadis declared war on the United States and tried to kill as many Americans as possible, we must be willing to listen to their own explanations. To do otherwise is to impose a Western interpretation on the extremists, in effect to listen to ourselves rather than to them.

Mary R. Habeck
*Knowing the Enemy*, 2006

The fundamental premise of the vast majority of scholarly examination, as well as public discourse, of the nature of America's enemy in the war against terrorism is that Islamic jihadism is based on Islam's grievances with various U. S. actions and policies in the middle eastern nations. This premise fails to truly identify the enemy and to rationally understand its nature. In truth, the conflict is not based on grievances at all, but instead is the result of a basic and fundamental incompatibility between the ideology of the Islamic jihadi and the basic, natural rights articulated during the European Enlightenment, assumed in American values, and encapsulated in the expression, "Life, Liberty, and the Pursuit of Happiness." The only way this incompatibility will be reconciled, given the U. S. and western civilization's deep and permanent adoption of the Lockean philosophy of tolerance, is for Islam itself to reform.

In the discussion that follows, the term "jihadi" will be used to collectively describe three distinct variants of Islamic reform ideologies whose adherents are commonly referred to as Islamic radicals, extremists, or terrorists. Yale University scholar Mary Habeck offers one of the most detailed descriptions of the term and its meaning.[1]

The first category of jihadis use as the basis of their ideology the transition from the first four righteous Caliphs, or holy leaders, to the hereditary monarchy known as the Abbasids, which occurred near the origins of the Islamic faith in the 7th and 8th centuries. Jihadis view hereditary and other rulers who do not rule by the laws promulgated by the earlier Caliphs, the sharia law, as apostates who are attempting to undermine Islam and destroy God with innovation and interpretation. These jihadis believe that Muslims must follow the example of the first four Caliphs and the learned religious leaders who followed them, the "salafi," and follow only sharia law.[2]

A second category of jihadi ideology focuses on Mustafa Kemal, also known as Ataturk, and the abolition of the Ottoman Caliphate on 3 March 1924. These jihadis believe that since the beginning of the Islamic religion, there has always been a sacred Caliph recognized by all of Islam, at the head of sharia law. The abolition of the Caliphate therefore made it impossible to fully implement sharia law, and consequently destroyed Islam. These jihadis believe that Muslims must restore the Caliphate, or continuously live in sin.[3]

The third school of jihadi thought maintains that falsehood and un-belief, or evil, has always attempted to destroy Islam since the beginning of the faith, through different manifestations during different epochs. Jews and Christians have always been chief among these manifestations, but other world religions periodically rank high as well. These jihadis view America, Europe, and Israel as the latest additions to forces constantly attempting to destroy Islam. In this world view, the decline and disorder in Islam is not the result of internal weaknesses or the sins of Muslims themselves, but instead is the work of external forces of evil. These jihadis believe that Muslims must destroy the manifestations of falsehood and un-belief in the world.[4]

A survey of the historical interaction of the United States with the Islamic world reveals the centuries-old and true nature of the present conflict. This history also reveals some lessons learned, and subsequently forgotten, particularly as they pertain to today's conflict. Islamic jihadism is not simply a result of that history, but instead has been an integral part of it for centuries. The real result of that history, specifically the general failure of Islamic cultures to advance, must be considered to prevent western leadership from adopting nearsighted grievance based views of the origins of modern Islamic terrorism. Such myopic views embolden Islamic jihadism through appeasement, rather than engage in rigorous examinations of its cultural causes and future solutions.

The Eighteenth Century – the Barbary Wars

The history of conflict between the United States and the Islamic world begins with the very founding of the North American nation in the late 18th century. A series of diplomatic and military engagements with the North African, or Barbary sheikdoms of Morocco, Tunis, Algiers and Tripoli occurred between 1784 and 1815, which became collectively known as the Barbary Wars. For centuries, these states, under the rule of sheiks, deys, or other strongmen, and under differing degrees of affiliation with the Ottoman Empire, filled their coffers not by honest sea-going commerce, but instead by operating a well developed and feared piracy system on the high seas of the Mediterranean and North Atlantic Ocean. This system included a steady

2

flow of forcibly taken vessels, their cargos, murder or enslavement of the crews of taken vessels, and a direct and significant flow of cash resulting from ransoms and the payment of tributes by the sea-going western European nations. Historians document that the Barbary piracy enterprise was integrated deeply with the Ottoman Empire's "white slave" trade and included seaside raids as distant as Iceland and Ireland, where the entire populations of small villages are known to have been "carried away" by Barbary pirates.[5] Significant to the U. S. conflict with the Barbary states, the Barbary piracy enterprise was also integrated into the prevailing "mercantile" economic system of trade exercised by the sea-going western European nations at the time of the American Revolution. For purposes of limiting or even eliminating the legitimate flow of commerce of competing nations, western European sea-going nations habitually entered into treaty and tribute paying arrangements with the Barbary deys rather than employing military force to destroy the sea raiders.[6]

In 1784, before the peace had even been settled with England, the Barbary piracy enterprise confronted the fledgling United States when Moroccan pirates hijacked the American merchantman "Betsy" in the Mediterranean and enslaved her crew. A year later, Algerine pirates seized two more vessels, the "Maria" from Boston and the "Dauphin" from Philadelphia, and enslaved their crews. The American ambassadors to England and France, John Adams, Benjamin Franklin and Thomas Jefferson, were able to oversee a negotiated peace treaty with Morocco. However, America and its statesmen had no real way to react to the larger demands of the Algerine leadership, given the young nation's bankruptcy, inability to raise a navy, and the weak central U. S. government associated with the Articles of Confederation.

After the adoption of the U. S. Constitution in 1788 established a new government, and after unsuccessfully ransoming more than 14 merchant ships and captured crews from Barbary pirates, President Washington eventually gathered in 1796 sufficient funds and political support to commission the construction of six warships. These six ships were intended to be the first United States Navy, and the fleet's first mission was to urgently protect American shipping traffic from the threats posed by the Barbary pirates.

Before the ships were ready to sail, President Adams decided to attempt to negotiate the peace and began a program of paying tribute and ransom, which initially yielded favorable results for the Americans. President Jefferson, however, resorted to military action in 1801, after more piracy and after Tripoli declared war on America. Beginning with a naval blockade in 1801, hostilities escalated until the famous 1804 naval bombardment of Tripoli. Lieutenant Stephen Decatur distinguished himself in this engagement, and the gallant Mr. William Eaton led the U.S Marine Corps in an attempt to replace the dey of Tripoli. The Tripolitan war resulted

3

in the successful ransom and release of the American hostages in 1805. The U. S. attempt at regime change in Tripoli, however, was unsuccessful.[7]

The freedom of American shipping and sailors did not last long. Embroiled in the hostilities between England and Napoleon's France, and in the resulting War of 1812 with England, President Madison found the Barbary pirates demanding more tribute, and now in collusion with the British navy. In 1812, Algerine pirates again began terrorizing American shipping, enslaving the surviving crewmen, and effectively stopping U.S. trade in the Mediterranean. Algiers declared war on the U. S. in 1812, and as soon as he was able, in fact one week after the Treaty of Ghent ended the war with England in 1815, President Madison dispatched a squadron of U. S. Navy frigates, under the command of now Commodore Decatur, to make war on the dey of Algiers. The U. S. squadron dealt significant damage to the Algerine pirate fleet shortly after entering the Mediterranean. Decatur was able to dictate terms of peace to the Barbary strongmen, for the first time in almost a generation. The settlement now included large reparation payments from Algiers, Tunis and Tripoli.[8] After thirty years, American shipping was no longer at the mercy of the Barbary pirates, and the American government was no longer strapped with exorbitant payments of tribute to buy an uncertain peace.[9]

While the Barbary Wars are commonly perceived to be a "sideshow" relative to other contemporaneous events such as the French revolution, the French Quasi-War, Napoleon's conquests, and the War of 1812, they warrant consideration because of their strategic significance to today's conflict. Franklin, Washington, Adams, and especially Jefferson and Madison, all believed that the Barbary Wars were a continuation of the American Revolution. Whereas the ground war in North America had freed America from Britain's tyranny, they believed the Barbary Wars were fought to win the same freedom of action and commerce within the international community, and specifically within the Atlantic Ocean and Mediterranean Sea trade routes.[10] The diplomacy, extortion of tribute and ransom, and the military actions of the Barbary Wars, to say nothing of the multitudes of slavery and imprisonment stories that appeared both in the western press and in U. S. government offices because of the Barbary Wars, "crystallized" the perceptions of the Islamic and Ottoman worlds in the minds of the founders and the American public at large. As opposed to romantic images and sometimes intentionally misleading information provided to the American colonists by the English, the Barbary Wars revealed to the U. S. the "despotic Turk" strongman as the antithesis of the early American republican identity, and generated much discourse of Islam as the antithesis of true religion.[11]

The founders saw three main issues within the Barbary Wars which necessitated victory to preserve what had been gained in the war for independence from Britain, and to permit the future success of the American experiment. First was the confrontation of piracy and free trade. After the peace was concluded in 1783, with England recognizing a free America, the Americans expected to find in the Atlantic the lucrative benefits of unfettered access to markets, and the respect due to the champions of free trade not just for the U. S., but for people everywhere. Instead, what America found with its first interaction with Islam was a world of terror on the high seas, lawlessness, and a world of tribute systems that amounted to nothing more than protection money.

The second issue was the confrontation between tyranny and freedom, and again, the continuation of the American Revolution. In adopting the U. S. Constitution, Americans established that power ultimately resided with the governed peoples, not in those who claimed to be the government. In contrast, what Americans found in the Barbary sheikdoms were "absolute rulers who gained power through bloody coups and wielded it through intimidation."[12] Washington and Adams referred to the Islamic leaders as "nests of banditti", while Jefferson's and Madison's campaign literature called them "petty tyrants."[13]

The third confrontation was between American "civil religion" and Islam itself. Though the historical record clearly indicates that Americans did not perceive the Barbary Wars as a conflict between Christianity and Islam, historians agree that religion was in fact a main issue. Rather than a confrontation of theological differences, to Americans this confrontation was about tolerance, religious freedom and more specifically, the nature of the societies the two ideologies generated.[14] The relevance of the Barbary Wars to the present war against Islamic jihadism can be seen through these same three main issues. Many of the autocratic or monarchic nations in the region today exhibit the same dependence on petrochemical dollars as they did to piratical tribute and ransom in the 18th century. Allowing this substitution for Barbary demands of tribute, almost nothing has changed in the 200 years between 1806 and 2006.

Much ignored in the modern historical assessment and literature regarding the period, is the fact that Islamic jihadi ideology was present and influenced the chain of events in the Barbary Wars. In a letter to John Jay while posted as the American Commissioner to France, Jefferson described a conversation he had with Ambassador Abdrahaman of Tripoli regarding the Barbary pirate attacks on U. S. shipping. Jefferson states he was told that all Christians are sinners in the context of the Koran, and that it was a Muslim's "right and duty to make war upon them wherever they could be found, and to enslave as many as they could take as prisoners."[15] Furthermore, the ambassador told Jefferson that Islam gave great incentive to the Barbary pirates to fight infidels because the Koran promised that making war against infidels ensured a Muslim paradise after death.[16] Jefferson's report of the jihadi motivations of Tripoli was not unique to the sheikdoms in the Barbary Wars. The same rationale was claimed for the Ottoman practice of "white" or Christian slave trading in captives from the Balkans, Caucasus and Ukrainian regions throughout the 18th century.[17]

Richard O'Brien, the imprisoned captain of the Philadelphia merchantman "Dauphin" and later the American consul to Algiers provided another account some years later. He related that his captor Ali Hassan, the dey of Algiers, considered Christians as the primary source of Algiers' riches. O'Brien wrote to American officials that Hassan had promised God he would extract all he could from Christians either through piracy or by extortion.[18]

While one may argue that these are anecdotal views of single individuals, the role that jihadi ideology played in the Barbary Wars is unmistakably documented by the explicit references to jihad and "Holy War" in the many and various treaties that Americans entered into with Muslim rulers. Tunis and Algiers, as the western outposts of the Ottoman Empire, even described themselves to American envoys as the "frontier posts of jihad against European Christianity."[19]

Nonetheless, the American founders went to great lengths to deny the religious and ideological nature of the conflict, especially to the Muslims themselves. The founders were quick to realize that the Barbary pirates were hypersensitized to the historic conflict between Islam and European Christianity, not only in the context of the Crusades, but much more recently in the context of the 16th through 18th century conflict to expel the Moors from Spain. They were quick to conclude as well that any religious conflict might jeopardize the commerce, free trade and free markets that America hoped to find in the Mediterranean. Further, the founders possessed a deep conviction for religious tolerance, and proudly explained in the short-lived 1797 Treaty with Tripoli that the U. S. was not a Christian state at all, but instead one with no official religion as well as laws forbidding the prohibition of religion.[20] The denial of the religious and ideological nature of the present conflict continues today, but has become the basis of a fundamental misunderstanding of the root of the conflict.

18th Century Islamic Reform – Toward a 7th Century "Paradise"

For a more complete understanding of the relation of the jihadi ideology in the Barbary Wars to the present conflict, American interaction with the Barbary sheikdoms must be viewed in the context of attempts to reform greater Islam in that period. Too many writers today assert that jihadism originated in response to 19th century European colonialism, or even from

6

grievance with various 20th century policies in the region.[21] Most scholars, however, commonly link the origins of modern jihadi ideology to the 18[h] century or earlier. Frequently, they describe the associated reform movements as "Islamic revivalism" when in many respects they are less "revivalist" and more "reactionary" to the perceived loss of Islamic political power that essentially paralleled the rise of the European Enlightenment in the west.[22]

Ibn Wahhab launched one such reform movement in 1744. Wahhab, with the backing of the Saud family of Arabia, set out with "uncontrolled rage" to violently purify the Islamic faith by returning to the authentic Islam of the pious founders of the religion (also known as the "salafi"). Wahhab prescribed jihad against heretics and the infidel as the only solution to bring Islam back to its original pristine medieval state.

The warlike reform spread rapidly and destructively and by 1802, the Wahhabi followers succeeded in sacking Karbala in present day Iraq, an event which continues to be mournfully commemorated due to the Wahhabi massacre of thousands of Shiite Muslims in their Karbala mosques. The jihadi ideology of the Wahhabis flourished at the time and threatened Ottoman control of significant areas of their empire, before Egyptian warriors crushed it on behalf of the Ottoman sultan. However, the Wahhabi faith has experienced several significant revivals during the intervening two and a half centuries, and subsequently continues to have tremendous influence over militant, political and jihadi Islamic ideology.[23]

Ibn Wahhab drew direct inspiration from another prominent Islamic reformer, Ibn Taymiyya, who preached in the 13th century, and espoused the puritanical call to use jihad to propel Islam back to the ways of the 7th century. Taymiyya advocated jihad on all who did not worship and believe properly (infidels and apostates), as well as on those who failed to rule by the holy law of sharia. Ibn Taymiyya is widely considered the foremost advocate of the jihadi ideology, and his theory of jihad continues to be revered in Islam as Ibn Taymiyya's major contribution to Islamic "law".[24] The influences of the medieval Ibn Taymiyya, as well as that of the contemporary Ibn Wahhab, on the Barbary sheikdoms are clearly expressed in Jefferson's report of Ambassador Abdrahaman's comments to Jay, and are visible in the many references to jihad in the treaties and other documents forwarded to the U. S. government by the Barbary strongmen.[25]

## The Nineteenth Century – Missionaries and Gunboat Diplomacy

Decatur's 1815 sweep of the western Mediterranean, which inflicted significant damage on the Barbary pirate fleet, and the ensuing treaty with Algiers, resulted in a peace that lasted for several decades. That is not to say that there was little meaningful interaction during the nineteenth century. On the contrary, the century saw considerable opportunities for the United States to learn about the true nature of the Islamic world and the potential for the development of the western nations' present adversaries within it. Barring several small squirmishes and interventions, an American policy of "armed neutrality" was the backdrop that succeeded in ensuring the safety of American merchant shipping in the Mediterranean, as well as establishing the environment favorable to a series of commercial treaties and free trade agreements. Nearly all of these agreements were amiably reached within sight of the masts of the American naval Men of War at anchor in the harbor.

Significantly, the "armed neutrality" stance of the U. S. underwent its first significant test in the first half of the century. In 1821 President John Quincy Adams was barely able to resist assisting the Greeks in their war of independence, when both the American and European publics urged war with the Ottoman Empire.[26] As America focused on westward economic expansion and its own internal political troubles, helping the Greeks win freedom and liberty was not worth the risk of compromising future Mediterranean commerce and the free trade treaty with Constantinople that had been considered a necessary goal since the 1780s.

During their presidencies, Jefferson and Madison advocated the view that a continuous American military presence in the region was necessary to protect U. S. national interests. This view gained nearly universal support after the War of 1812 in the form of establishing a "Mediterranean Squadron" of the U. S. Navy. However, in 1831 President Andrew Jackson at long last secured a treaty of amity and free trade with the entire Ottoman Empire.[27] The Turkish Treaty of 1831 ultimately prompted the Secretary of the Navy to report in 1838, naively, that "the causes which originally dictated the policy of employing a portion of our navy in the Mediterranean have in great measure ceased."[28] Within a few years events allowed him to withdraw the squadron, only to be forced to reestablish it less than three years later. Reminiscent of decades before, the reestablished Mediterranean Squadron was again tasked to protect American merchantmen from Ottoman privateers, who this time carried letters of marque against American vessels, issued in response to the American war with and invasion of Mexico in 1847. From 1861 to 1866, while the U. S. struggled to excise its great moral cancer of human slavery, the American Mediterranean Squadron diminished to only one small vessel, a corvette named after one of Washington's original Barbary frigates, "Constellation."[29] With the resumption of trade after the American Civil War, the squadron returned to the Mediterranean.

As might be expected after such a traumatic experience as the American Civil War, when America returned its attentions to the Mediterranean, U. S. relations with the Ottoman Empire became less commercial and returned to a focus on concerns for the natural law and natural rights espoused by the founders.  This resulted not exclusively from the trauma of the Civil War, but also from significant changes in the policies of the Ottoman sultanate itself.  In fact, the last three decades of the 19<sup>h</sup> century saw the Islamic world assume a patently anti-Christian and anti-Semitic posture that tested the U. S. resolve to follow its "armed neutrality" policies.  Despite growing pressures from the European powers to implement modernizing reforms of the archaic, corrupt, and theocratic Ottoman sultanate, the Ottoman Empire became more intolerant and openly oppressive of Christian and Jewish minorities as the empire continued the process of its disintegration through the end of the 19<sup>th</sup> century.

As early as the 1840s, President Martin Van Buren began expressing concern publicly and diplomatically for the plight of Jews in "the most anti-Semitic of countries," the Ottoman Empire.[30]  In 1875 this type of Western concern was dramatically renewed.  In that year, uprisings and the Ottoman condoned mob-murders of the French and German consuls in Serbia, together with the unsuccessful invasion of Christian Abyssinia with Egyptian troops, alarmed Americans and Europeans alike.  Nearly simultaneous to these Ottoman actions, the Ottoman sultan, Abdul Hamid, beleaguered and troop-constrained by insurrection and impending border wars, mobilized irregular forces to pacify Bulgaria.  The result became known as the "Bulgarian Horrors", a massacre of nearly sixty thousand Christians and Jews.  The Ottomans maintained, in a convoluted fashion, the massacre was the result of American and Russian instigated sedition.[31]

Fearing the outbreak of war and the safety of the many American citizens in the Ottoman Empire, President Ulysses Grant dispatched six warships of the U. S. Mediterranean Squadron to Constantinople and the surrounding waters.  The force remained highly visible there for many months and many Americans and Europeans in the city became convinced that its presence was the only thing that kept them safe.  The U. S. managed to remain free of entanglement in the subsequent Ottoman wars with England and Russia by refraining from military intervention in the successful Bulgarian revolution, and by considerable diplomatic and commercial maneuvering, until the crisis abated. [32]

Again in 1882, President Chester Arthur ordered the entire Mediterranean Squadron to Alexandria, Egypt to assist in evacuating Americans and Europeans in view of riotous and chaotic massacres of Christians reported in the city.  With the arrival of more than 40 ships of the British, French, and U. S. Navies, and the evacuation of the majority of the remaining European and American Christians, the situation was gravely complicated by the Egyptian warlords' seizure of the Suez Canal, the Egyptian and Ottoman shares of which were sold for cash to British Prime Minister Disraeli in 1875.  After 10 days of negotiations with Cairo and

9

Constantinople, the British fleet issued an ultimatum which was not heeded, then commenced bombarding the city and its fortifications the next day. The Americans did not join in the action until two days later when the Egyptian defenders abandoned the city, lawless and in flames. The U. S. Marine Corps was the first to go ashore with the intention of re-opening the U. S. consulate in order to signal their continued neutrality, but instead were fully employed fighting fires and looters for the two days before British Marines occupied the city. Because of the lack of order in the city before and after the siege, the scope of the 1882 massacre in Alexandria has never been determined. An interesting aside is that in the ensuing battles with Egyptian forces, the British reportedly found many U. S. Civil War veteran mercenaries among the ranks of the Egyptian troops and officers.[33]

The trend of growing atrocities with declining retribution seems to have reached the extreme case in 1894-5, when the tragedy that was the Ottoman sultanate now focused on exaggerated or even fictitious claims of conspiracy amongst the Christian population of Armenia. The massacres in Armenia, in terms of bloodshed and the amount of property destroyed, "made the Bulgarian Horrors seem of small account."[34] By now, however, the commerce, as well as the public and political focus of America, was completely in the west and the western Pacific, instead of the economically, politically and morally bankrupt and disintegrating middle east. In response to the 1894-5 Armenian atrocity, President Grover Cleveland proposed a cooperative Anglo-American intervention, but in the end no international action was taken at all.[35]

There were, however, small scale U. S. Navy and Marine Corps interventions in 1903 and 1904 which signaled the beginning of the end of U. S. isolation and reluctance to be involved on foreign territory. In 1903, an assassination attempt on the American counsel to Beirut in the midst of anti-Christian rioting caused President Theodore Roosevelt to send Marines into the city to help the Ottoman strongman there restore order. Several months later the Mediterranean Squadron put the same Marines ashore in Tangiers to force the local strongman there, a bandit named Raisuli, to release without ransom the Greek businessman Joseph Perdicaris, whom he had kidnapped with some bloodshed from U. S. Consulate there.[36]

By far, the most significant intercourse between the United States and the Islamic world during the 19th century was not the limited and highly cautious military interactions described above, but was instead the non-governmental, direct and widespread influence of the flood of American missionaries which began in 1819.[37] The American missionaries in the Islamic world quickly realized that proselytizing and evangelism was not productive with Muslims, largely due to the sharia law proscribing execution of Christian converts, who were considered apostate.

Consequently, American missionary efforts in the 19<sup>th</sup> century became focused on encouraging modernizing reforms in Islam, and in particular educational institutions.

Tolerance of religious diversity was the main message, but the missionaries had different levels of success in the two areas.  The "Hatti Serif of 1839", for example, was a decree obtained from the Ottoman sultan which was initially celebrated by American missionaries as universal religious freedom, until they realized it applied only to foreigners, not the indigenous Muslims and Eastern Orthodox Christians they intended to liberate from oppression.[38]

Substantially more success and influence was achieved in the area of education.  The establishment of Roberts College in Constantinople and the Syrian Protestant College (later the American University) in Beirut in mid-century resulted in highly successful, popular, and respected learning institutions that taught the basis of the European Enlightenment into the 20<sup>th</sup> century.  The focus on much needed education gradually caused a secularization of the American missionary effort in the Islamic world.[39]

This secularization and the armed neutrality of the American military presence in the region together presented a marked contrast to the self-interested colonial image of the European powers in the 19<sup>th</sup> century Islamic world.  According to Islamic historian and scholar Ussama Makdisi, the American missionary impact on secularism and education, combined with widespread knowledge of American immigration success stories, contributed to the "dramatic ascendancy" of the idea of the "Benevolent America" in the minds of 19<sup>th</sup> century Muslims.[40]

Other scholars, however, extracted a different conclusion from studies of the copious reports and documents the American missionaries sent back to the U. S., the world's most significant record of conditions and events in the 19<sup>th</sup> century Islamic world.

> When the first missionaries sent by the ABCFM (American Board of Commissioners for Foreign Missions) set off from New England early in the nineteenth century, the Ottoman Empire was about to enter a period of protracted reorganization and reform....Of all the principles and abstract ideas on which reforms were based, the equality of all the sultan's subjects before the law regardless of the religious background was perhaps the most difficult to approach and then put into practice.[41]

One student of the missionaries' written legacy, Jeremy Salt at Bilkent University in Ankara, Turkey, has published a detailed analysis of the American missionary experience.  Contrary to the bulk of modern scholarly assessment, Salt demonstrates that the historical record of the 19<sup>th</sup> century Islamic world is rife with well documented anti-Christian and anti-Semitic policies aimed solely at the persecution and subjugation of Christian and Jewish minorities by the Islamic majority.  Not only were the missionaries themselves subject to frequent and sometimes violent ostracism and retribution, but they frequently called upon

American diplomats to help obtain U. S. military assistance to intervene in extreme cases of Christian and Jewish persecution.[42]

The first cries of atrocity in the Bulgarian Horrors, the Alexandria and Armenian massacres, as well as the best military intelligence of the situations, for example, came from the American missionaries. In direct opposition to Makdisi's "Benevolent America," Salt claims the missionaries' records show that despite outspoken Muslim advocacy of the American missionaries' educational secularism, the public execution of converts and acolytes was common, even in areas near the universities.[43] Similar observations of feigned Ottoman friendship to U. S. diplomats and naval officers, while simultaneously discretely combating the Protestant and Catholic missionaries are also documented by James Field and Anne Venzon.[44]

## 19th Century Islamic Reform – Jihadism & the Growth of the 7th Century Dream

Clearly, 19th century western pressures for civil reform in the Ottoman Empire and the larger Islamic world were ineffectual. Meanwhile, the 19th century effort to reform and "revive" Islam continued the 18th century trend of reactionary movements intended to return the Islamic culture back to the sharia law and theocratic caliphate of the salafi, the pious 7th century founders of the Islamic religion, which was the violent cause of Ibn Wahhab.

The first of the two most influential reformers in the 19th century, Ibn Fudi, established himself as the caliph, or head, of the "Sokoto Caliphate" after declaring and successfully waging jihad in northwestern Africa in 1806. Ibn Fudi preached that Islam was plagued by two closely related problems, the injection of practices and ideas of "un-belief" into the Islamic faith not in accordance with the ways of the salafi, and the resulting social injustice.[45] Like Wahhab, Fudi believed that all "innovation", forward looking or otherwise, was an abomination to Islam. Accordingly, during his twelve year rule, the erudite Fudi espoused that to be Muslim meant that one must seize power in one's community, and compel the rule of Islamic sharia law over all inhabitants. He directed that followers of true Islam should not participate in commerce with un-believers, should befriend, comfort or assist them in no way, and were obligated to wage jihad on them to the extent of one's capability.[46] Modern jihadis combine Fudi's guidance with a well-known saying of Muhammad that "war is deceit", to conclude that true Muslims are also obligated to speak ambiguously, mislead, and lie to un-believers.[47]

The second of the influential 19th century reformers of Islam was Ali Sanusi, who was born near Algiers and educated in Fez, Morocco, and Mecca. Between 1840 and his death in 1859, he build about two dozen schools or headquarters from which he dispatched missionaries of his cause into Tripoli and Egypt. Less confrontational than Wahhab or Fudi, Sanusi's contribution to salafist jihadi thought was to reiterate Taymiyya's medieval warning that the Muslim sin of failing to wage jihad on un-believers is second only to the error of waging jihad on fellow Muslims. Sanusi focused his ministry on the concept of eliminating the blind "imitation" of Islamic scholars, or Imams, because the interpretive errors of their rulings, and the influence of un-believers on their religious rulings, have accumulated over the centuries to lead Muslims away from the faith of the salafi founders.[48]

Like the feigned reforms of the Ottoman Empire, the absence of forward looking reform within Islam during the 19th century was indicative of a widening gap between the contemporary progress of the European Enlightenment and the continual movement of Islamic religious leaders to "reform" toward the jihadi movement of the 20th century. The 19th century's trend of the Islamic leadership's inability to focus civil and religious reform to guide Muslims toward tolerance, personal responsibility, the rule of law, and America's novel idea that governments rule at the consent of the governed, resulted in the continued growth and the broader acceptance of the reactionary, intolerant, coercive, anti-Semitic and anti-Christian Islamic jihadi ideology.

## The Twentieth Century – Love, Hate, and War

Enormous amounts have been written about the history of 20th century interaction between the U. S. and the Islamic world that have proposed and advanced the idea that Islamic jihadism is rooted in Muslim grievances with the United States of America. The purpose of the preceding discussion of 18th and 19th century interactions was to demonstrate that such interpretations fail to account for the long history and roots of jihadism within the Islamic faith.

For example, scholars like Ussama Makdisi attribute the widespread sentiment of a "Benevolent America" that existed in the early 20th century Islamic world to several factors. Among these factors were the tremendous American educational efforts in the region, the unprecedented American famine relief efforts following World War I, as well as several American presidents' successful efforts to distinguish the U. S. from the ambitious and colonial European powers.[49] Despite this widespread sentiment, many scholars have erroneously marked the post-World War I partition of the ungoverned territories of the collapsed Ottoman Empire as the origin of the Islamic jihadi movement.[50] That theory, that the Islamic world would be a tolerant, prosperous contributor to the global environment today if the victors of the First World War had supported the Ottoman Empire, has become a popular premise in the literature and the media accompanying the rise of jihadism in the 20th century. One prominent and frequently referenced collegiate text book presenting this theory further asserts that present day

Islamic unrest is the direct result of the early 20th century actions of a single man, Winston Churchill.[51] A more recent work, but perhaps equally as acclaimed, espouses the same World War I theory but spreads the blame more liberally around the early 20th century British Cabinet, especially the foreign minister Lord Arthur Balfour.[52] Such theories of 20th century grievances ignore at least two centuries of disintegration of the Islamic culture and growth of the jihadi ideology within Islam, as the history of U. S. interaction with Islam outlined previously revealed.

The strenuous efforts of America to avoid interfering in Islamic affairs, while remaining unmolested by them, known in the 19th century as the "armed neutrality" policy, continued until World War II. When asked why he never asked Congress to declare war on the Ottoman Empire as they had on Germany and Austria-Hungary, President Wilson stated that he did not want to risk a new anti-Christian and anti-Semitic massacre, as the Muslim Turks had again perpetrated in 1915 in Armenia.[53] While President Wilson and his King-Crane Commission initially disagreed with the partition of the former Ottoman Empire, the administration quickly deferred to European interests in the region.[54]

Pre-World War II contact was primarily commercial, but the 1933 contract for Saudi Arabian oil development resulted in an exponential post war expansion of U. S. strategic interests there. In the ten years following World War II, for example, American commerce in the region increased more than 167%. The following decade (1955-1965) saw another 226% rise, and 321% again during the decade after 1965, in absolute terms.[55] During the Cold War, "armed neutrality" was clearly no longer sufficient to protect U. S. strategic interests anywhere, let alone in the Islamic world. America quickly assumed a decidedly "pro-Arab" policy during the period with the aim of limiting Soviet influence in those countries.

An example of President Eisenhower's "pro-Arab" policy was the U. S. defense of Egypt against Israel, France and the United Kingdom in the 1956 Suez War. Many conflicts occurred in the 20th century Islamic world to which America still remained neutral, but in 11 of the 12 major conflicts between Muslims and non-Muslims, Muslims and secular forces, or Arabs and non-Arabs, the United States provided support for the former group.[56] The single exception to this rule is Israel, which has been under attack continuously since 1948. Regardless, U. S. interaction with the Islamic world has become fashionable to describe as "anti-Islam", and is commonly cited as a likely basis for terrorism and jihadism. Barry Rubin, editor of *The Middle East Review of International Affairs*, articulately describes the revisionist history that is popular in literature and media:

> Indeed, internal conflicts in the Arab world have posed impossible dilemmas for U. S. policymakers. When the U. S. helps friendly governments such as Egypt's or Saudi Arabia's, it is accused of sabotaging revolutionary movements against

them. As soon as Washington starts to pressure Arab governments into improving their positions on democracy or human rights, however, it is accused of acting in an imperialist manner. If Washington did nothing and friendly regimes were overthrown, the radical conquerors would be unlikely to show any gratitude for U. S. neutrality...During Iran's 1979 revolution, for example, although Washington clearly wanted the shah to survive, it nonetheless restrained him from taking tougher actions to save his throne. And once the revolution had succeeded, President Carter then sought to conciliate the new Islamist government. (It was American contact with moderates in the new regime, in fact, that provoked the seizure of the U. S. Embassy in Tehran in November 1979.) And even though relations subsequently soured, Washington has never seriously tried to overthrow the Islamic government; on the contrary, it has periodically sought détente with Tehran. In fact, the only time the United States has ever become directly involved in a dispute between a government and Islamic revolutionaries was in Afghanistan during the Soviet occupation – and in that case, Washington backed the rebels.[57]

During the six decades since the abandonment of the "armed neutrality" policy in favor of a "pro-Arab" policy, perhaps the most significant trend in the history of America's involvement in the Islamic world is the increasing degree of friction between the natural rights espoused by the founders and U. S. foreign policy in the region. This friction has become part of a self-perpetuating cycle that feeds the jihadi propaganda effort both in the west and within the Islamic world. Despite the consistency of the "pro-Arab" policy discussed above, the policy meant that America frequently found itself supporting the anti-democratic, or even occasionally the outright corrupt, side in the described conflicts in order to ensure the safety of the continued flow of the region's oil to support the U. S. and the international economies.

In many cases, such as in the case of Iran's 1979 revolution, when conflicts appeared not to immediately jeopardize American economic interests, America attempted to remain neutral. U. S. assistance to multinational jihadi fighters to expel the Soviets from Afghanistan, and the defense of Israel from the 1973 attacks of its neighbors, are perhaps the only exceptions to this generalization. In the later case, America even prevented Israel from destroying its attackers. The end result is substantial U. S. support for repressive regimes like Egypt, Saudi Arabia, and Jordan, while the U. S. government and the media come dangerously close to equating Israeli settlements in Gaza and the West Bank with jihadi terror attacks.

The friction between the U. S. "pro-Arab" policy and the aims of the American founders is exemplified by this example. Israel is the only democracy in the region, where some 17% of the population is Muslim, where Muslim representatives are elected to a real parliament, and where the basic civil liberties of Muslims are legally guaranteed. Israel lost these territories in 1948 when Egypt and Jordan launched military assaults and forcibly occupied the Gaza Strip and the West Bank, but recovered them again in 1956. Significantly, the Muslim standard of living in

15

Gaza and the West Bank is more than ten times that of Egyptian or Jordanian Muslims, yet the U. S. government refers to these Israeli lands as "occupied territories."[58] It is this type of historical confusion and revision in western thinking that presents the single greatest challenge to developing a U. S. strategy to counter the threat of jihadism.

A second specific example of the friction between the U. S. "pro-Arab" policy and the aims of the American founders leaps from the study of corruption and foreign aid conducted by Alberto Alesina and Beatrice Weder. Their detailed and objective empirical study revealed that there is not, and has not been for decades, any statistical difference between the amounts of American foreign aid provided to corrupt versus non-corrupt regimes, despite the advertised policies of the U. S. of the last decade to support non-corrupt democracies.[59]

### 20th Century Islamic Reform – Jihadism: Unprecedented Anti-Semitism and America as the Focus of All Blame

Historical confusion and revision, together with the misrepresentation of American aims, also play substantially in the modern academic assessment of 20th century reform within Islam itself. The reactionary jihadi ideologies of reformers like Sayyid Qutb in Egypt and his successor Usama bin Laden in Saudi Arabia have had great success leveraging 20th century western advances in mass media to garner widespread exposure of their messages to the Islamic world, resulting in the reality that today jihadism is no longer a small part of the Islamic world.[60]

One author in the journal *Parameters*, estimates that the madrassas, or private Islamic schools, in Pakistan alone produce more than one million young men a year, educated in the jihadi ideology, who have killed thousands of innocent Christians and Jews, as well as Muslims, who control several Islamic countries, and who possess a dominant influence in several others.[61] In her brilliant book *Knowing the Enemy*, Habeck documents how Qutb and bin Laden spread their message that the decline of Islam is not the result of flaws within Islam itself, but is instead the deliberate effort of America and the Jews. The message of these reformers, that jihadis must blame Americans and Jews for all evils suffered by Muslims around the globe, has entered into mainstream Islamic thought and dialogue.[62] The misunderstood historical nature of this grave problem is manifest in the literature and the U. S. government by the common and politically correct description that "militants," "extremists," "radicals," and "Islamists" have "hijacked" the "peaceful" religion of Islam, when jihadism is in fact a scourge that Islam fosters and accepts. However, as will be discussed in the next section, there are a number of modern Islamic states that struggle to counter the spread of jihadism by embracing some or many of the principles of the European Enlightenment.

Another area of considerable discourse that presents evidence of the widespread passive acceptance of jihadism in Islam is the debate on democracy as a viable solution for the inequities and corruption in the Islamic world.  The supposition of many scholars is that democracy in the Islamic world will lead, as in Iran in 1979 for example, to an authoritarian or theocratic jihadi regime.[63]  This view relies on the premise that if the election process is legitimate and uncorrupted, the majority of Muslims will support jihadi regimes.  While the argument supports the idea of widespread passive acceptance of jihadism, it overlooks the absence of many other products of the European Enlightenment that must accompany democracy in order to create a civil society, such as tolerance, free markets, rule of law, and property rights.

This supposition, that democracy is not a viable solution for the inequities and corruption in the Islamic world, is a main teaching of the 20th century reformers Qutb and bin Laden.[64]  In opposition to the convictions of the American founders, and the underpinnings of the European Enlightenment, it implies that not all people are endowed with the natural right to freedom from coercion and the liberty to improve their lives.  Instead, it implies that some are more suited to lives of oppression.  The contrary viewpoint, despite the widespread acceptance of jihadi reforms within 20th century Islam to return to the 7th century ways of the salafi, that democracy does in fact improve the lives of Muslims just as it does for Christians, Jews, Buddhists, and Hindus, is best made by the objective assessment of real world conditions:

> Islam is not inconsistent with democracy.  The majority of the world's Muslims live in democracies, in Indonesia, Bangladesh, India, Turkey, the Balkans, Mali, etc.  However, it would be foolish to ignore that of the 22 Arab states there are no democracies, and only three (in the Gulf and Morocco) guarantee effectively even a few basic liberties such as relative freedom of the press.  Recently the "Arab Human Development Report, 2002" by a brave group of Arab intellectuals to the UN Development Program has indicated some of the reasons for this situation:  Approximately half of Arab women are kept illiterate; there are only one-fifth as many books translated into Arabic every year as are translated in Greek; Arab per capita income has shrunk to a level just above sub-Saharan Africa.  Bernard Lewis pointed out not long ago that the 22 Arab states plus Iran (together approximating the population of the U. S.) export less to the world than Finland.[65]

Columbia University's Richard Bulliet agrees that democracy is the hope that Islam will overcome jihadism.[66]  Habeck and Aslan more strenuously argue that democracy is essential to counter the jihadi objective to eliminate democracy, and is essential in creating governments more responsive to their citizens.[67]

The Success of the American Experiment; The Failure of Islamic Reform

Islamic jihadism is not a contemporary historical anomaly that will ultimately prove to be a strategic distraction, or "presentism," as described by strategist Colin Gray.[68]  The demonstrated jihadi skill at manipulating the western mass media, combined with the imminent jihadi access to weapons of mass destruction, force jihadis to the forefront of strategic importance.[69]  Jihadism has been growing for centuries, accelerating as the Islamic empire and its power waned, and will continue to threaten civilization until it is checked.  Islamic jihadism originated coincident with much of the European Enlightenment, which achieved a pinnacle with the founding of the United States of America.  At its core, Islamic jihadism is a violent rejection of many of the fundamental principles of the European Enlightenment.  Democracy, free markets, tolerance and freedom of religion, secular government, and separation between the religious, the political, and the individual are simultaneously the cause of the Islamic jihadi's religious fury and the European Enlightenment's propulsion of western civilization's quantum advances in the human condition.   It is no coincidence then, that Islamic jihadis, under the banner of cleansing their religion of evil western influence, have focused their attentions on the U. S., the very manifestation of the European Enlightenment, and which has achieved so much success and progress exercising the very principles that Islamic jihadis despise.

The failure of the Islamic world to incorporate the advances in thought and civilization that resulted from the European Enlightenment has caused the stagnation, or even the decline, of that culture over the last several centuries.  The successful incorporation of these same advances in thought and civilization into the very fabric of government and society in the U. S. has directly resulted in the greatest and most rapid improvements in the human condition ever observed by history.  This applies not just to the North American continent, but to the global population as a whole.  The only Islamic nations which have prospered since the 18th century are the ones that have embraced, in some fashion, the western principles of democracy, free markets, property rights, tolerance, and the rule of law.  Islamic jihadis, however, believe just the opposite.  They see the stagnation or the decline of their culture as a result of Islamic communities or leaders succumbing to the temptation of these same principles, which they see as evil and contrary to the beliefs of true Muslims.

Perhaps the most onerous example of the 20th century's neglect of the historical religious basis of jihadi terrorism, is the absence of the objective assessment of the failure of the Islamic world to improve the human condition of its populations, particularly in contrast to the dramatic success of American implementation of the achievements of the European Enlightenment, and the impact of the global spread of these achievements on global human well being.  Jared

Diamond, in his book *Guns, Germs, and Steel*, repeatedly emphasizes the fundamental biological reality that for populations to grow, they must increase the lifespan of individuals by reducing early death from disease and violence, or increasing the fertility rate through improved nutrition. The improvements in fertility rates, reduction in disease and death by warfare, and staggering improvements in global nutrition, have transformed a human race whose population was nearly stagnant before the European Enlightenment into a thriving and flourishing species whose growing numbers threaten overpopulation in several areas of the globe.

Before the year 1650, for example, the global population was 500 million with a doubling time of almost 2000 years, all the way back to the dawn of civilization. After 1650, with fundamental changes occurring in technology as well as the way humans governed themselves, both results of the European Enlightenment, the global human population doubling time quickly collapsed to less than 150 years. At the end of the Second World War in 1945 the global population of 2.5 billion doubled in a period of 127 years. This sort of population flourishing is not possible, according to Dr. Diamond, unless human beings are better nourished, have less disease, and less violence. [70]

After WWII, the doubling time of the global human population again significantly declined to 50 years, and presently, with a global population of 7 billion, the doubling time is less than 39 years. Coincident with this improvement in the global human condition, the number of democracies operating under the rule of law in 1945 was 22, representing 16% of the global population. In 2005, 120 democracies represented 60% of the global population. [71] Supporting Dr. Diamond's assessment of well being, during the same period chronic undernourishment in developing countries reduced from 37% to 17%, and global retail prices of flour, potatoes, and cured meat, relative to per capita income, declined 92%, 82%, and 85% respectively. [72]

The success of the European Enlightenment at improving the human condition is by no means universal. The Islamic world, which through centuries of reactionary reform has produced the jihadi ideology that systematically rejects the advances in civilization produced by the European Enlightenment, is among the regions with the least improvement in the human condition. As observed by Bernard Lewis,

> By all indicators from the United Nations, the World Bank, and other authorities, Muslim countries – in matters such as job creation, education, technology, and productivity – lag ever further behind the west. Even worse, the Arab nations also lag behind the more recent recruits to western style modernity, such as Korea, Taiwan, and Singapore. [73]

Comparatively, all nations in the Islamic world in 2006, except Qatar, Bahrain, Kuwait, Oman and Turkey, which have recently adopted significant free market and democratic reforms, rank in the bottom half of nations in productivity as measured by manufactured goods per capita. Only Morocco, Indonesia, Saudi Arabia and Bangladesh are in the 3rd quartile.[74] According to the World Bank, the average per capita income of all Islamic nations collectively is less than half of the average for the globe, and according to the United Nations, Kuwait is the Islamic nation with the longest life expectancy, which is near the global average.[75] In other words, all other Islamic nations are ranked in the 3rd or 4th quartile in terms of life expectancy.

In a rigorous analysis of empirical data available from the United Nations, Wheaton College business professor Seth Norton has proposed a cause for the type of widespread human deprivation found in the Islamic world and described above. In a statistical regression analysis, Norton demonstrated a compelling correlation that strong property rights, one measure of the rule of law, significantly reduce the deprivation of the world's most impoverished people. Weak property rights increase that deprivation. Specifically, Norton found an almost absolute correlation between the U. N.'s mortality rate measure, the percentage of a population that dies at age less than 40 years, and weak or absent property rights. Of nations with weak rights, the mortality rate exceeds 25%, while in nations with strong rights the rate is less than 6%. Not surprisingly, there is no statistical correlation between the mortality rate and the U. N.'s assessment of the availability of health care. Strong correlations also exist showing that strong rights result in one fourth the illiteracy rate and a six-fold reduction in the proportion of a population without access to potable, unpolluted water.[76]

In summary, to claim that America, the west, and the advance of the ideas of the European Enlightenment across the world, as jihadis and many in the media and literature have, is somehow detrimental to humankind denies the reality of the world that one can measure. The example metrics cited above underscore this conclusion. Stated in another way, the assertion that human conditions in the Islamic world are acceptable or even desirable as do jihadis, their supporters and apologists, condemns a large fraction of the human population to hopeless deprivation. The historical and scientific misrepresentation that allows such claims and assertions demonstrates the absence of objective analysis and critical thinking in the discussion of grievance based Islamic jihadi terrorism. Accordingly, one of the greatest challenges facing strategic leaders today is objectively examining the centuries-old roots of Islamic jihadism, and developing a strategy that will lead to a lasting solution to the western conflict against it.

## Conclusion and Recommendations – Strategic Communications, Public Education, and the Greater Good

Thus it is Islamic jihadism's rejection of religious tolerance, democracy, and the rule of law, in favor of a virulent anti-Semitism, of theocracy, and of sectarian strongmen exempt from law and privileged by the authority they have usurped, that is the real enemy in America's centuries-long interaction with the Islamic world. It is essential that the grand strategy of the United States addresses this basic conflict of interests, rather than as though the present conflict is new, is not a religious conflict, or is the result of the religion itself having been "hijacked" by rogues. These aspects of the conflict must be confronted and addressed.

It is not, as Thomas Friedman argues in *The World is Flat*, that the fruits of the American Experiment, free markets, property rights, tolerance, democracy, and the rule of law, have left Islam behind.[77] On the contrary, it should be clear now that it is Islam that has opted out of progress, by allowing, promoting, and embracing centuries of reactionary and retrospective reforms that rejected the idea that humans can indeed improve their condition through reason and rationality. Islamic clerics and the kleptocrats who act as leaders in much of the Islamic world need to understand that they are in fact responsible for the condition and grief of their people.

Domestically, America must revitalize the education of its public in what is known simply as "civics." The broader the audience that understands what is truly generating Islamic jihadism, the broader the spectrum will be of potential approaches and solutions to the international problem. Education at all levels should inculcate U. S. citizens in the history, philosophy, mechanics, virtues, responsibilities, and achievements of the western approach to freedom, liberty, the free market, and what tolerance and diversity really mean, rather than the versions that accept oppression and tyranny. Such an effort would entail reinstalling this subject matter into the curricula of the schools where it was long ago removed. This should be a large-scale full-spectrum effort that should not be left solely to bureaucrats. Instead the strategic leadership of the nation should drive the public education effort, much as the founders did in the 18th century. The *Federalist Papers*, generally attributed to James Madison, Alexander Hamilton, and John Jay, are prototypical examples of effective strategic communications which aimed, among other things, to create a government strong enough to defend itself against the Barbary pirates.[78] U. S. strategy should strongly encourage this sort of revitalization of public education in the history and principles of western culture, and its performance in terms of human well being, internationally as well. What is recommended, essentially, is an information operations campaign aimed at promoting the global greater good.

Internationally, U. S. foreign policy needs an overhaul to reflect U. S. national values and long term objectives, rather than near term expediencies devoid of the principles enumerated by the founders. In general, American foreign policy should be reformed to address the ineffectiveness of U. S. foreign aid programs that Alesina and Weder have documented.[79] America should set a highly visible international standard by supporting non-corrupt democracies, rather than funding kleptocracies that violate many principles of the rule of law, grow because of the revenue, and flourish to become the next security problem. Additionally, rather than providing foreign aid to provide short term stability in governments where power is already centrally concentrated, America should more strenuously promote trade and development in Islamic nations supporting the rule of law, tolerance, and democracy. Trade and development in these nations empowers people and entrepreneurs, causes economic progress, and helps decentralize power in a culture that has deep tendencies toward autocracy and kleptocracy.[80]

Bernard Lewis summarizes the importance of promoting freedom and the decentralization of power in the Islamic world:

> To the Western observer, schooled in the theory and practice of Western freedom, it is precisely the lack of freedom – freedom of the mind from constraint and indoctrination, to question and inquire and speak; freedom of the economy from corrupt and pervasive mismanagement; freedom of women from male oppression; freedom of citizens from tyranny – that underlies so many of the troubles of the Muslim world.[81]

A specific first step in U. S. foreign policy reform, which is suggested by the historic interaction between America and the Islamic world, is to abandon Eisenhower's "pro-Arab" policy as a relic of the Cold War. America must confront the fact that it compromised many of its founders' principles in order to defeat Bolshevism and communism. To defeat Islamic jihadism, it is now more necessary than ever for the U. S. to return to its founders' principles in its relations with the Islamic world, as was the general case in the 18th and 19th centuries. Accordingly, the "pro-Arab" policy has served its purpose and is now a liability.

In a new grand strategy for the greater good, America should actively marginalize Islamic nations that are not supportive of the development of the rule of law, tolerance, and democracy. Inversely, the U. S. should ardently and visibly support nations in the region, such as Israel, that seek peace, prosperity, and the improved well being of their citizens. To do otherwise fuels the rhetoric of Islamic jihadis that America's policies seek to oppress Muslims throughout the world, and fuels the oppression and injustice that history indicates is the cause of widespread passive support for the ideology.

The overwhelming obstacle to abandoning the Cold War's "pro-Arab" policies, of course, is the tribute-like dependence of developed nations on oil, which fosters and supports many of the region's kleptocracies. A necessary co-requisite to this important first step to defeat Islamic jihadism, therefore, is for the West to embark on an ambitious, courageous and radical program to redefine how its economies obtain and distribute energy. Former Director of Central Intelligence R. James Woolsey asserts that denying Islamic jihadis the use of oil as a weapon against America and the West must be America's highest priority.[82]

Separate from nationally targeted foreign policy, strategic leaders of the U. S. and the West must confront the reality that Islamic jihadism is a religious phenomenon that has grown popular and powerful enough to threaten the continued progress of the American Experiment and the European Enlightenment. In the new grand strategy to defeat Islamic jihadism, America must campaign, through its scholars and theologians if appropriate, to encourage and facilitate Imams and other Islamic religious authority figures to reform Islam itself in a forward direction, one that breaks from the past and encourages tolerance, the rule of law, free inquiry, and free markets. Imams in the West as well as in the Islamic world that passively or actively support Islamic jihadism must be undermined and exposed, using logic and reason, as supporters of a decaying ideology that will never lead to improved well being for adherents to the Islamic faith. In the turbulent internal conflict that Islamic scholar Reza Aslan explains now embroils the Islamic religion, America and the West must support the forces within Islam that stand for future progress:

> Despite the tragedy of September 11 and the subsequent terrorist acts against Western targets throughout the world, despite the clash-of-civilization mentality that has seized the globe and the clash-of-monotheisms reality that underlies it, despite the blatant religious rhetoric resonating throughout the halls of governments, there is one thing that cannot be overemphasized. What is taking place now in the Muslim world is an internal conflict between Muslims, not an external conflict between Islam and the West. The West is merely a bystander – an unwary yet complicit casualty of a rivalry that is raging in Islam over who will write the next chapter in its history.[83]

Finally, the history of American interaction with the Islamic world demonstrates repeatedly over two and a half centuries that "diplomacy backed by force", a term coined by former U. S. Ambassador to Algeria, Lebanon, and then Morocco Richard Parker, is the only effective approach to relations in the Islamic world pending the grand strategy changes that are recommended in the preceding paragraphs.[84] Diplomacy is essential to ensure intentions are understood. Consistent diplomacy is essential to build the trust that the Islamic world needs to support America's aims in advancing the ideals of European Enlightenment. Military weakness and the inability to project American national power, throughout the history of the interaction between the United States and the Islamic world, has consistently caused Islamic jihadists and kleptocrats to launch opportunistic attacks against the interests of the United States.

Endnotes

[1] Mary R. Habeck, *Knowing the Enemy, Jihadi Ideology and the War on Terror,* (New Haven, Connecticutt: Yale University Press, 2006), 9-13.

[2] Habeck, 9-10.

[3] Habeck, 11.

[4] Habeck, 12-13.

[5] Bernard Lewis, *The Middle East, A Brief History of the Last 2,000 Years* (New York: Simon & Schuster, 1995), 175.

[6] Frank Lambert, *The Barbary Wars, American Independence in the Atlantic World* (New York: Hill & Wang, 2005), 106-109.

[7] Richard B. Parker, *Uncle Sam in Barbary, a Diplomatic History* (Gainesville, Florida: University Press, 2004), 103-130; and Lambert, 49-78.

[8] Kevin Baker, "The Shores of Tripoli," *American Heritage* 53, no. 1 (February/March 2002): 21.

[9] Parker, 128; and Lambert, 181-193.

[10] James A. Field, "Novus Ordo Seclorum," in *America and the Mediterranean World 1776-1882* (Princeton, NJ: Princeton University Press, 1969), 3-26; and Frank Lambert, "The American Revolution Checked," in *The Barbary Wars, American Independence in the Atlantic World* (New York: Hill & Wang, 2005), 15-28.

[11] Ussama Makdisi, ""Anti-Americanism" in the Arab World: An Interpretation of a Brief History," *Journal of American History* 89, no. 2 (September 2002): 539-540.

[12] Lambert, 106.

[13] Lambert, 110, 123.

[14] Lambert, 106, 112-114.

[15] Thomas Jefferson, "The American Commissioners' Report to John Jay," in *The Works of Thomas Jefferson* 9, ed. Paul L. Ford (New York, 1904), 358; quoted in Lambert, 116.

[16] Thomas Jefferson, "The American Commissioners' Report to John Jay," in *The Works of Thomas Jefferson* 9, ed. Paul L. Ford (New York, 1904), 358; quoted in Lambert, 117.

[17] Lewis, *The Middle East*, 175.

[18] Lambert, 110-111.

[19] "The Truce with Tunis," *Naval Documents Related to the United States Wars with the Barbary Powers* 1 (Washington, D. C., 1939), 158-159; quoted in Lambert, 117.

[20] Parker, 134-135.

[21] An example of this short term view is Richard W. Bulliet, "The Crisis within Islam," *The Wilson Quarterly* 26, no. 1 (Winter 2002): 13.

[22] Lewis, *The Middle East*, 310.

[23] Reza Aslan, *No God But God, The Origins, Evolution, and Future of Islam* (New York: Random House, 2005), 240-245.

[24] Habeck, 20-28.

[25] Jefferson, 116-117; and Lambert, 110-111.

[26] James A. Field, *America and the Mediterranean World 1776-1882* (Princeton, New Jersey: Princeton University Press, 1969), 133-140.

[27] Field, 148-151.

[28] Field, 209.

[29] Field, 306.

[30] Field, 345-373.

[31] Field, 364-367.

[32] Field, 368-370.

[33] Field, 430-435.

[34] Field, 446.

[35] Field, 445-447.

[36] Anne Cipriano Venzon, "Gunboat Diplomacy in the Med," *Proceedings of the U.S. Naval Institute* (April 1985): 26-31.

[37] Makdisi, 538-545.

[38] Jeremy Salt, "Trouble Wherever They Went: American Missionaries in Anatolia and Ottoman Syria in the Nineteenth Century," *Muslim World* 92, no. 3-4 (Fall 2002): 296.

[39] Makdisi, 544.

[40] Makdisi, 543.

[41] Salt, 287.

[42] Salt, 311.

[43] Salt, 287-313.

[44] Field, 430-447; and Venzon, 26-31.

[45] Ahmad Dallal, "The Origins and Objectives of Islamic Revivalist Thought, 1750-1850," *Journal of the American Oriental Society* 113, no. 3 (July-September 1993): 352.

[46] Dallal, 354.

[47] Habeck, 124.

[48] Dallal, 357.

[49] Makdisi, 544-5.

[50] Makdisi, 546.

[51] David Fromkin, *A Peace to End All Peace, The Fall of the Ottoman Empire and the Creation of the Modern Middle East* (New York: Henry Holt, 1989), 23-62.

[52] Robert Fisk, *The Great War for Civilization, The Conquest of the Middle East* (New York: Alfred A. Knopf, 2005), 305-315.

[53] Fromkin, 259-260.

[54] Makdisi, 549.

[55] Bernard Lewis, *The Crisis of Islam, Holy War and Unholy Terror* (New York: Random House, 2003), 126-128.

[56] Barry Rubin, "The Real Roots of Arab Anti-Americanism," *Foreign Affairs* 81, no. 6 (November-December 2002): 75.

[57] Rubin, 74.

[58] R. James Woolsey, "Grand Strategy in the Middle East: The Long War of the 21st Century," in *An American Grand Strategy for the Middle East*, ed. K. M. Campbell (Washington, D. C.: Aspen Institute, 2004), 37.

[59] Alberto Alesina and Beatrice Weder, "Do Corrupt Governments Receive Less Foreign Aid?" *American Economic Review* 92, no.4 (September 2002): 1126-1138.

[60] Richard W. Bulliet, "The Crisis within Islam," *The Wilson Quarterly* 26, no. 1 (Winter 2002): 15.

[61] Michael G. Knapp, "The Concept and Practice of Jihad in Islam," *Parameters* 33, no. 1 (Spring 2003): 92.

[62] Habeck, 12.

[63] Four examples of thoughtful discussions on the supposition that democracy in the Islamic world leads to jihadist theocracy or autocracy are Audrey Kurth Cronin, "How al-Qaida Ends, The Decline and Demise of Terrorist Groups," *International Security* 31, no. 1 (Summer 2006): 43; James Kurth, "America's Democratization Projects Abroad," *The American Spectator* 39, no. 8 (October 2006): 40; Larry P. Goodson, "Things Change and Things Stay the Same:  New Realities and Underlying Constants in the Middle East," (Carlisle Barracks, Pennsylvania: n.p., 2006); and Edward Walker, "The Middle East:  Policies for the Coming Decades," in *An American Grand Strategy for the Middle East*, ed. K. M. Campbell (Washington, D. C.: Aspen Institute, 2004), 26.

[64] Aslan, 138; Habeck, 162; and Lewis, *The Crisis of Islam,* 159.

[65] Woolsey, 31.

[66] Bulliet, 19.

[67] Aslan, 253-263; and Habeck, 177.

[68] Colin S. Gray, "Stability Operations in Strategic Perspective:  A Skeptical View," *Parameters* (Summer 2006): 4-14.

[69] Audrey Kurth Cronin, "How al-Qaida Ends, The Decline and Demise of Terrorist Groups," *International Security* 31, no. 1 (Summer 2006): 39-41.

[70] Jared Diamond, *Guns, Germs, and Steel, The Fates of Human Societies*, (New York: W. W. Norton, 1997), 83-93.

[71] ADM Michael Mullen, USN, "64th Annual Pearl Harbor Day Commemoration," speech at the USS Arizona Memorial, 7 December 2005, *Navy Office of Information*, Washington, D. C.; available from http://www.pearlharbormemorial.com/site/pp.asp?c=fqLQJ2NNG&b=1313503; Internet; accessed 2 December 2006.

[72] Indur M. Goklany, *The Improving State of the World:  Why We're Living Longer, Healthier, More Comfortable Lives on a Cleaner Planet* (Washington, D. C.: Cato Institute, 2007).

[73] Lewis, *The Crisis of Islam,* 114.

[74] James Gwartney, Robert Lawson, and William Easterly, *Economic Freedom of the World, 2006 Annual Report* (Vancouver: Fraser Institute, 2006), 39.

[75] Lewis, *The Crisis of Islam,* 113-119.

[76] Seth W. Norton, "Poverty, Property Rights, and Human Well-Being:  A Cross-National Study," *Cato Journal* 18, no. 2 (Fall 1998): 239-243.

[77] Thomas L. Friedman, *The World is Flat, A Brief History of the Twenty-First Century* (New York: Farrar, Straus, and Giroux, 2005), 470-479.

[78] James Madison, Alexander Hamilton, and John Jay, *The Federalist* (New York: Random House, 1937).

[79] Alesina and Weder, 1126-1138.

[80] Iqbal Z. Quadir, "The Bottleneck is at the Top of the Bottle," *The Fletcher Forum of World Affairs* 26, no. 2 (Summer/Fall 2002): 86-88.

[81] Bernard Lewis, *What Went Wrong?  The Clash Between Islam and Modernity in the Middle East* (New York: Oxford University Press, 2002), 159.

[82] Woolsey, 33-34.

[83] Aslan, 248.

[84] Parker, 160.

www.ingramcontent.com/pod-product-compliance
Lightning Source LLC
Chambersburg PA
CBHW081810280526
45789CB00008B/3076

9 781500 623326